OLD DULVERTON
and

Dulverton — Bury — Brushford — Exebridge

A pictorial and historical record
written and compiled by

Hilary Binding

and

Victor Bonham-Carter

The Exmoor Press

First published 1986

ISBN 0 900131 49 7

MICROSTUDIES

Each Microstudy has been written by an expert or experts, and is designed to appeal to all who are interested in Exmoor.

The Editor of the Series is Victor Bonham-Carter

A list of all the titles is available from
The Exmoor Press   Dulverton   Somerset

Printed in Great Britain by Williton Printers, Williton, Somerset

Contents

Illustrations

The source of each photograph, where known, is indicated on the relevant page.

Front Cover picture of Barle Bridge is by J. H. German.

Inside Front Cover Map was drawn by Clery Welch.

The photograph of Aubrey Herbert, MP, on page 19 is by courtesy of John Murray, publisher; and of Dulverton Friendly Society banner on page 78 by courtesy of the *Western Morning News*.

Dulverton before 1914.

German.

1 Early History

Dulverton is inseparable from Exmoor. Geographically the southern 'gateway' to the National Park, the town is situated in the deep valley of the Barle, about a mile above the confluence with the Exe, and is enclosed on three sides by steep wooded hills. It has in turn, and for centuries, served the people of the surrounding hill country as a fording place, refuge, and commercial and administrative centre. As a border manor of the Royal Forest of Exmoor, it was frequently mentioned in medieval documents in connection with fines imposed for the illegal slaughter of deer and other irregularities, also in the records kept of the perambulations of the Forest boundary. Today the civil parish covers an area of 3,538 acres, with a population of 1,300, while the town itself provides a range of shops and services both for local people and visitors, as well as housing the administrative headquarters of the Exmoor National Park Authority.

Dulverton (originally 'dieglaford'—the hidden ford) began as a small settlement serving those who crossed the river Barle at this safe site. It also offered a sheltered and secure retreat behind the defences of Oldberry Castle, Mounsey Castle, and Brewer's Castle upstream, hill fort enclosures built in Celtic times to control tribal movements. Several ridgeways converge on Dulverton, and we can envisage it as a place where, from earliest days, travellers could rest and provision in comparative safety.

During the 11th century Dulverton belonged to the aristocratic Saxon family of Godwin, notably to Harold, Earl of Wessex, who succeeded his father in 1053, was elected King in 1066 and killed at the battle of Hastings in that year. Dulverton then passed into the hands of William the Conqueror, who granted the smaller manor of Potesdona (Pixton) to Roger de Corcelle. The details of landholding were already complex when recorded in Domesday Book in 1086, and so they continued throughout the Middle Ages, with Dulverton and its adjoining manors being granted in turn and in part to various lords, no one family establishing itself in the area for long. Linked first with the Turberville family; then—in the 1200s—followed a series of complicated land grants and exchanges involving the Pyn family and the much-married Hawisia, which eventually culminated in the whole of the manor of Dulverton being granted to Taunton Priory by 1340.

By this date, with sheep grazing the rough hill pastures, it is likely that at least one mill had been built in the town, and even a fulling mill

Barlynch Priory was a small community of Augustinian canons founded in the 12th century. Some of the original stones are visible in the present farmhouse and outbuildings. One of the bells in Dulverton Church is said to have come from Barlynch.

V.B-C.

as well—all part of a thriving woollen industry. Trade in general was growing. In 1306 Edward I had granted the lord of the manor a licence to hold a market each Thursday and an annual fair for three days over the Feast of All Saints. Dulverton market was a convenient outlet for the sale of cattle and farm produce, while the fair attracted outsiders who came to buy wool and other local merchandise, and to sell a variety of goods unobtainable in the locality—necessaries such as salt, and luxuries such as silks for those who could afford them. In 1488 new arrangements were made, whereby the Prior of Taunton was empowered to hold two fairs a year: one on the Feast of SS. Peter and Paul on 11 July and the other on the feast of SS. Simon and Jude on 6 November, each lasting three days and each having a 'Court of Pie Powder'—the 'dusty feet' or peripatetic tribunal for the settlement of claims and disputes arising at the fair.

Following the dissolution of the monasteries—at which time the tiny priory of Barlynch, about two miles north-east of the town and already bankrupt, was quietly liquidated—the manor of Dulverton had by 1540 reverted to the Crown, and so remained until 1556 when it was sold to William Babington, a member of the Privy Council, for the sum of £1,230 5s. By this time the town was in a sorry state, with no clear leadership emerging in the troubled times. In response therefore to a plea of poverty, the Crown (Philip and Mary) issued a fresh licence in 1555 to ten 'goodmen' of Dulverton to hold the weekly market and the two annual fairs, which had lapsed. The ten citizens, some of whose names still sound familiar (Sydenham, Chilcote, Tout and Venn, variously spelled, among them), were given powers to renew their membership and required to use the fees and profits 'for the advantage of the tenants and inhabitants of the town'.

In 1568 the manor was sold again, this time to John Sydenham, one of the 'ten', whose family was already well established in the neighbourhood (see chapter 2). A survey showed how sizeable the manor had become:

Eighty messuages, twenty cottages, twenty tofts, six mills, six dovecotes, eighty gardens, thirty orchards, two thousand acres of land, one hundred acres of meadow, two hundred acres of pasture, three hundred acres of wood, two hundred acres of gorse and heath, one hundred acres of woodland, and a hundred shillings rent in Dulverton, Pyxton, and Combe.

In the following century, as elsewhere, Dulverton was involved in religious and political controversy: notably in 1641 when Parliament required every adult male—under oath of loyalty to King Charles I—to sign a Protestation 'to maintain and defend . . . the true Reformed Protestant Religion, expressed in the Doctrine of the Church of England, against all Popery and Popish Innovations . . .' The parish constables were responsible for collecting the signatures and returning the lists of those who had signed and those who had not (the 'recusants') to the sheriffs. The Dulverton list was signed by 226 persons over the age of 18. Among those who failed or refused to sign, or who were later accused of opposing Parliament in the Civil War that followed, were two names of note. One was that of John Byam, parson of Clatworthy, who was also vicar of Dulverton. The penalty for recusancy was sequestration of property or the payment of a heavy fine. Byam lost out at Clatworthy but resisted successfully at Dulverton on the grounds that he had already conveyed the incumbency to someone else. The other name was that of Henry Sydenham (descendant of John), who admitted that he had been 'in arms' against Parliament. In consequence he had to pay up—in his case 10 per cent of the value of his personal possessions valued at £200; but he did not lose his property at Dulverton.

After the Restoration in 1660, small groups of Dissenters began to organise secret meetings, and in due course built their own places of worship under licence from the Bishop of Bath and Wells.

A plan of the manor made in 1792 for the Sydenham estate shows a crowded town centre with a variety of unfamiliar street names. The middle of Fore Street was built over and narrow roads—King Street, Queen Street, and Broad Street—crept between the houses. The Rectory lay behind The Green, while the Vicarage and Vicar's Orchard lay between the Church, the Town Marsh, and the present garden area north of Rosemary Lane. Throgmorton and Milham Lanes lay where

Duck Paddle (Chapel Street) is today. The woollen industry, in decline during the 1500s, had been revived; and coarse woollen cloth and blanketings were being manufactured. Attempts had been made to exploit lead and silver deposits at Combe by a Derbyshire company; ore was carried by packhorse to Minehead and then shipped to South Wales, but the venture did not last long. Copper was also worked at Combe for a while, while limestone was quarried and burnt at Gulland. A tanyard stood out beyond Woodliving on the road to Minehead, and survived until the 1840s.

Manorial courts still met regularly in the 18th century to hear complaints about nuisances and the upkeep of roads and property. Officers were still being appointed in 1765, though their duties were often nominal: constables, tythingmen, searchers and sealers of leather, a bread weigher, ale tasters, and keepers of the pounds. Only Thomas Browne, clerk of the market and fairs and his successors, were kept fairly busy, for the income from these events was a useful source of public revenue. In 1732, for example, profits from the fairs paid for a fire engine! In 1750 an offer was made to draw on the market account and contribute 30 shillings per quarter to the salary of Thomas Matthew, the charity schoolmaster, plus £1 for furnishing the school premises. The offer, however, was respectfully declined. Money had been left to establish this school in 1715 where boys were 'to be taught to read' and girls 'to net and sow' (sic). Other jobs that can have been no sinecure related to the

persons appointed to watch in the night-time within the Town and Burrough of Dulverton, on any extraordinary occasion or otherwise, in order to prevent and see (if possible) any accident that may happen to ye inhabitants of the sd town by ffire or otherwise, which sd persons are to watch two at a time.

A list of couples follows and it is good to note that women took their turn to watch alongside the men.

Money from parish funds and private charity was also devoted to the assistance of the 'industrious poor', at a time when most paupers were afforded relief at home. A parish poorhouse was however maintained in Church Lane, but reserved probably for the aged and incapable. It was not until the Poor Law Amendment Act 1834 that the 'able-bodied' poor were herded into workhouses, where conditions were made deliberately inferior to those of the meanest labourers outside. The workhouse at Dulverton was not built until 1855—nineteen years after the passing of the Act—at a cost of £2,811 plus £675 for the site. John Hall and his wife, the first master and matron, were paid annual salaries of £25 and £15 respectively, with free lodging and weekly rations in kind. The first medical officer was Dr. C. P. Collyns, author of the classic, *Notes on the Chase of the Wild Red Deer*.

Dulverton Workhouse

German

Apart from the resident population of paupers, tramps would arrive in the evening for board and lodging. They worked next day, sawing wood or breaking stones, and then stayed another night before moving on to Tiverton, South Molton, or Williton. A 'bread and cheese' station was kept by the Denscombe family in a cottage near Brompton Regis where, on the production of a ticket, a roadster would receive sustenance. The ration was weighed out exactly.

The properties of the Manor of Dulverton were dispersed after 1818 to a variety of private buyers, many of them former tenants of the Sydenhams, while the manor itself was assigned in 1858 to the Earl of Carnarvon. A plan of the town in 1820 reveals a more familiar Dulverton. Street names have taken their modern form, although there is still a shambles in Fore Street and a Market House, two shops and a butter cross nearby, which mark the site of the original market place. The end of the manor was the beginning of Dulverton, more or less as we know it today.

Combe, seat of the Sydenham family at Brushford, c. 1590.

Sydenham

View of Combe from the east, c. 1907.

Bedwell

2 Landed Families

We have now reached the 19th century when, under the impulse of the Industrial Revolution, the urban population was rising fast and power was passing from the landowners to the manufacturers. Nonetheless the countryside continued to be dominated by the landed families, especially round Dulverton.

Sydenham

In 1322 one John Sydenham—who came from Bridgwater—married Mary, daughter and heiress of John of Peekstone or Pixton; and it was their second son, Hugh, who inherited or was given the property by his mother. How extensive Pixton was at that time is not known, nor how long the Sydenhams owned it. Meanwhile other Sydenhams had settled elsewhere in the area. In 1482 Edward Sydenham married Joan or Jane, daughter of William of Combe in the parish of Brushford—an historic house that stayed with the family until its eventual sale in 1874. The present building is mainly Tudor in character; but it incorporates portions of an older house and has been extensively altered, both within and without. At one time, for example, there was an enclosed courtyard on the east side, entered by an archway through which carriages were driven. The old engraving reproduced opposite gives a fair impression of the exterior after rebuilding in c. 1590.

Tradition has it that Sir Francis Drake, who married Elizabeth Sydenham (of Combe Sydenham, Monksilver) as his second wife, played bowls at the Brushford house. Certainly a couple of Armada medals and several Elizabethan coins were discovered during excavations beneath the front porch, which give a clue to the rebuilding. A silver candlestick, hallmarked 1750, was made out of ore mined on the estate and was known to be in family hands in the 1920s. A rather tall story survives from the same period when Major George Sydenham, the then owner of Combe, used to have arguments with his friend, Captain Dyke, about the existence of God and a future life. It was agreed that whoever died first should return three nights after the funeral to speak to the other, who must however sleep in the little garden house at Combe. The Major duly died first, and so Captain Dyke took up quarters in the garden house where he slept undisturbed. Several weeks later, however, when asleep in another room, he

11

was woken by a ghostly visitant whom he recognised as his old friend.

> He came and drew my bed curtains aside, saying 'Cap, Cap . . . I could not come at the appointed time. I come now to tell you that there *is* a God, a very just and terrible one. You will find it so if you do not turn over a new leaf.'

As related earlier, the Sydenhams owned numerous properties in Dulverton, where they were lords of the manor between 1568 and 1858. During that time several members of the family made a modest mark on history. In the Civil War loyalties were divided. Humphrey, a fluent preacher, known as the 'silver-tongued', and an ardent supporter of Charles I, was deprived of his livings by the Parliamentary commissioners and lived in retirement at Combe until his death in 1650. Thomas, the 'father of English Medicine', sided with Parliament but was captured by the Royalists at Exeter in 1643 and served a term in prison. During the plague of 1655 he retired to a safe place and wrote a treatise on curing fevers, and subsequently a 'celebrated' description of gout, which caused him much affliction. His son, Henry, bore arms against Parliament as noted.

In the 18th century another Humphrey lost £20,000 in the South Sea Bubble, of which sum £18,000 had been secured against the manor of Dulverton. Fortunately for him, his losses were recouped when he came into the St. Barbe property in 1722. Humphrey was a benefactor as well as a gambler. It was he who founded the charity school in Dulverton in 1715 and kept it going until his death in 1757, when he left £100 for the continued instruction of poor children, while his daughters added £50. Within a few years, however, according to a worried note left by the 85-year-old schoolmaster, the fate of the capital seemed in doubt, which may account—as in so many other cases—for the disappearance of the charity and the school. A relative of the family, Floyer Sydenham, gained fame as a scholar, notably for his four-volume commentary on the works of Plato. Unhappily he fell into poverty, was arrested for a small debt in 1787 and died in prison. It was his death that prompted his great friend, the Rev. David Williams, to found the Literary Fund (later Royal) which has since become the principal authors' charity in Great Britain.

The last of the Sydenhams to live at Combe was the Rev. Charles St. Barbe Sydenham (1823-1904). He was the prototype of the educated Victorian parson, who buried his talents in the country as priest and 'father of the parish'. He spent 57 years at Brushford—11 as curate to his father who died in 1858, and 46 as his successor as rector. He was proud of the fact that, during his working life, he spent no more than

Brushford Church and Rectory. The field in foreground has probably been limed.

German

30 days away from the parish. There are memorials to him and his family in the church and churchyard.

The connection with Dulverton was sustained for another generation by his son, George Francis, who was born at Combe in 1861, qualified as a doctor in 1884-5, and practised in the town, living at Battleton House. Apart from medical duties, he was a churchwarden, magistrate, keen amateur archaeologist and local historian, also delighting in fishing and cricket. He was chiefly responsible for the compilation of the massive family history, from which much of this information is taken*. Since his only son died on active service in 1916 in Mesopotamia, he was the last male Sydenham at Dulverton, dying on 18 March, 1924. See his photograph on p. 34. As at Brushford, there are several family memorials in All Saints Church and churchyard, and a family vault near the north wall close to the north door.

---

*The History of the Sydenham Family. Privately published 1928.

13

Acland

Pixton came to the Acland family as part of the dowry of Elizabeth Dyke on her marriage in 1745 to Sir Thomas Acland, 7th Baronet. This made the Aclands one of the largest landowners in the west, with four estates in Somerset (Holnicote near Selworthy, Pixton near Dulverton, Tetton near Taunton, and Petherton Park near Bridgwater), and one at Killerton, the main family home near Exeter in Devon. As Anne Acland relates in her book, *A Devon Family* (Phillimore 1981), Holnicote and Pixton 'included stretches of the finest staghunting country in England'. Moreover, although the Aclands of the 19th and 20th centuries were public-spirited men, who cared deeply for their land and tenants and employees, and were only incidentally interested in sport, the two Baronets who reigned between 1745 and 1794 thought of very little else.

Sir Thomas the 7th was particularly well placed to indulge his passion for hunting, in his combined role as Warden of Exmoor Forest (some 20,000 acres of moorland centred on Simonsbath), which he leased from the Crown and where deer had been hunted since Saxon days; and as Master of the North Devon Staghounds, forerunners of the 'Devon and Somerset'. Thus he took full advantage of the lie of his properties, with hounds kennelled at Holnicote in the north of the Moor, and at Highercombe and Jury in the south. Likewise he kept open house at both Holnicote and Pixton, each being fully furnished and equipped with linen and plate for limitless hospitality on hunting days. To quote Anne Acland:

Pixton was the larger establishment (73 tablecloths in 1759, including eight new ones 'of the largest size'), but each of them had a silver dinner service of five dozen plates and any number of tankards, cups, bowls, dishes and salvers, used not for ornament but for actual eating and drinking, as the scratches on the plates still testify.

In 1770 Sir Thomas settled Pixton (and Tetton and Petherton Park) on his eldest son, John, on the latter's marriage to Lady Harriet Fox-Strangways. Thereafter he conducted his hunting from Holnicote, which was burned down—for the first time—in 1779, the second occasion was in 1851. But this was a time of tragedy, for John died at Pixton in 1778. He had been wounded and taken prisoner by the Americans in the War of Independence and nursed by a brave wife, who crossed the lines under a flag of truce to do so. His death occurred after a stupid and inconclusive duel, not from that cause, but from the after-effects of war wounds and general ill-health. That was not the end of Lady Harriet's troubles, however. Her father-in-law died in February, 1785, followed two months later by that of her small seven-year-old

River Haddeo and Packhorse Bridge at Bury, before 1914.

German

son, another John. The unhappy widow stayed on at Pixton until her daughter, Elizabeth Kitty, married the second Earl of Carnarvon in 1796. She then retired to Tetton where she survived until 1815. Her name is remembered today by the carriage drive, now a bridleway, beside the River Haddeo between Bury and Wimbleball Lake, constructed in the days of her widowhood to give easy access from Pixton up to outlying parts of the estate near Wiveliscombe.

The title had meanwhile passed to old Sir Thomas's second son, another Thomas, who became 9th Baronet (little John had been the 8th), who was , it seems, a spendthrift. He had already got through so much money that his father decided to tie up the family resources and allow him a modest income only. But the two men resembled each other in their passion for staghunting, and in their open-handed hospitality to friends and followers. Sir Thomas the 9th kept house at Holnicote and Highercombe, and his activities as Master of the Hunt were plentifully recorded in the diaries of Parson Boyse, incumbent of Hawkridge-cum-Withypool, himself a hunting maniac. This Sir Thomas did not live long. In 1785 he had the good sense to marry a rich and strong-minded wife, Henrietta Hoare, who bore him two sons and two daughters before his death in 1794. That was the end of the Acland hunting saga, and the start of a new era of responsible landownership under the 10th and 11th Sir Thomases, whose lives spanned the 19th century. And, as from 1796, it was the end of the Pixton connection too.

Herbert (Earls of Carnarvon)

The chief seat of the Earls of Carnarvon, when they acquired Pixton by marriage in 1796, was—and is today—Highclere Castle in Hampshire. The acquisition merely increased the holdings of a family already well endowed with land, and bore a close resemblance to what had happened in 1745 when the Aclands added Pixton to their various estates. And so, until the coming-of-age of Aubrey Herbert (1880-1923), a younger son of the fourth Earl, Pixton was regarded by the Carnarvons as their 'sporting estate in the West Country', and not as their principal home.

In her biography of Aubrey Herbert, *The Man who was Greenmantle* (Murray 1983), Margaret FitzHerbert makes clear that the Carnarvons were not only wealthy landowners, but often eccentrics in the best English tradition, who supported unusual causes and travelled tirelessly about Europe and the Middle East, where they attracted a host of friends of different nationalities and interests. Aubrey combined these characteristics with—from early youth—a genuine love of Pixton in preference to any of the other Carnarvon houses: which no doubt was why his mother (his father's second wife) presented it to him, together with half the Exmoor estate, when he reached the age of 21 in 1901.

Pixton house—a building in the classical style—is described by Margaret FitzHerbert:

> It was a large 18th century house, with Victorian additions, of great charm but no architectural distinction. Set high on a hill amidst magnificent trees in a deer-filled park, it soon became a magnet for Aubrey's friends. There were many house parties. Edward Cadogan wrote of them years later, 'I look back to these bachelor parties as among the happiest experiences of my existence.'

The bachelor existence lasted until Aubrey's marriage in 1910 to Mary de Vesci, who had to cope, not only with her formidable mother-in-law, but with the vast scale of entertainment sustained at Pixton. Indeed Pixton continued to attract numerous guests of every sort—though on a less lavish scale—until the end of the Herbert reign in the 1970s.

That Aubrey and Mary truly made Pixton their home, and had the interests of the estate and neighbourhood at heart, was demonstrated by the royal welcome they received on their return from honeymoon on 12 November 1910. According to Margaret FitzHerbert:

> The people of Dulverton, Bury, Brushford and Kings Brompton had made elaborate preparations for this homecoming. The tenantry of Pixton were feudally exuberant. A committee and two sub-committees, one for lighting and one for decoration, were formed. Detonators had been placed along the railway track which were discharged by the approaching train to warn the waiting crowd of the imminent arrival. The station was decorated with streamers and flags and laurel bushes. A carpet and triumphal arch

Pixton House, south front, before 1914.

Dulverton Band.

Lock

German

saying *welcome* were on the platform. Amidst loud and prolonged cheering Aubrey and Mary descended from the train and walked between a guard of honour formed by the Royal Devon Hussars to their carriage. There, the white horses had been taken out of the shafts and ropes attached, so that the carriage could be pulled by the tenantry and employees of Pixton Estate. A torchlit procession formed, led by the Dulverton Brass Band, followed by the two led carriage horses, unencumbered of their load, then four mounted Hussars, then the carriage dragged by tenantry, then more mounted and unmounted Hussars, then the Dulverton boy scouts, then the station-master and assistant station-master and bringing up the rear a huge crowd, singing, cheering and, according to the local paper, 'emitting hunting cries'. All this rowdy enthusiasm was apparently undampened by a prolonged downpour. Bedraggled but still cheering they made the one and a half mile journey to Pixton, up the station drive to the house, where more illuminated arches bearing messages *God bless the happy pair, Thine own wish wish I thee* and other such sentiments greeted them.

In the following year, after two earlier defeats, Aubrey won Yeovil (then called the South Somerset Division) for the Conservatives in a Parliamentary by-election, and he held the seat until the end of his life. But his over-riding interest in public affairs was fixed on the Balkans where, in the wars of 1912-13, Turkey was expelled after nearly 500 years, except for the eastern corner of Thrace. Aubrey had been honorary attaché at Constantinople in 1904-5 and, after subsequent travels and adventures, he had made many friends among the Turks and learned to speak their difficult language. This enabled him to play a unique role during the 1914-18 war when, for example, at Gallipoli on 25 May, 1915, he organised an eight-hour truce to clear the battlefield of thousands of rotting corpses; and, in the following year, when he tried—unsuccessfully as it turned out—to negotiate honourable terms for the British surrender at Kut-el-Amara. Aubrey's war and post-war career was so extraordinary that it has to be studied in detail to appreciate his contribution to events. Suffice it to say here that this brilliant and erratic man, crippled with near-blindness, died of septicaemia following a dental operation on 23 September 1923 at the early age of 43. He is commemorated in the north chapel of Brushford parish church, designed by Edwin Lutyens: containing a recumbent effigy with sword under a wooden canopy.

After her husband's death Mary Herbert became a Roman Catholic and brought up her children in that faith, her son Auberon going to school at Ampleforth. She also fostered an R.C. congregation at Pixton, where Mass was said in a prefabricated hut, known as the 'iron room', until a permanent church, dedicated to St. Stanislas, was opened in Dulverton in 1955. At the outbreak of the second world war, Auberon was at Oxford, but from then on his career assumed a striking resemblance to that of his father. What Turkey (and Albania, whose independence he had espoused) had meant to Aubrey, Poland meant to Auberon. Rejected by the British Army for his flat feet, Auberon was accepted by the Polish forces and served as a private until commissioned towards the end of the war, taking part in the invasion of Normandy with the 1st Polish Armoured Division. During and after the war, he championed the cause of the Polish Government in exile. He spoke Polish and several other East European languages; and opened Pixton and houses in London as places of refuge, not only for Poles but for others whose countries had been overrun.

Among all these foreign tangles, Auberon did not forget home affairs. He stood characteristically but unsuccessfully as a National Liberal for Parliament, and was devoted to Dulverton where he served, first on the old Rural District Council, and then on the West Somerset District Council; also on the National Park Committee before and after re-organisation. He was a keen sportsman, an unorthodox rider to hounds, and he ran an excellent pheasant shoot at Pixton. Like his father, he combined acute intelligence with wit and the ability to get on with everyone, duke or dustman. He died unmarried in 1974, and with his death Pixton passed out of direct Herbert ownership.

Aubrey Herbert, M.P., campaigning at Yeovil.

Murray   19

Beague—Mildmay

Hollam, thought once to have belonged to the Sydenhams, lies in the woods a mile or two ENE of Dulverton, off a long narrow lane and a short distance below the source of the Hollam Brook. In the early 18th century Hollam was owned by the Heard family; but in 1750 the last Heard daughter married a Beague, who was descended from a branch of the French family of Le Bégue and known to have emigrated to West Somerset during the previous century. According to *Kelly's,* a Miss Beague was in residence in 1861. However that may be, the property had passed in 1858 to Charlotte Mary, daughter of Charles Heard Beague, Lieutenant in the Royal Engineers, who died in 1883. Charlotte Mary married twice: first to Major Douglas Halkett, who was killed in the Charge of the Light Brigade in 1854; secondly to Arthur George St. John Mildmay, whose family had owned the manor of Queen Camel in East Somerset since 1554. Mildmay was an officer in the 86th Regiment and political adviser to the Maharajah of Bikanir. Charlotte accompanied him to India and shared the perils of the Indian Mutiny in 1857-8.

In due course they returned to make Hollam their permanent home. Their son, Charles Beague Mildmay, born in 1861 and educated at Marlborough and the Royal Military Academy, Woolwich, was gazetted to the Royal Artillery in 1880, and to the Royal Horse Artillery in 1884. He served in the South African War 1900-1. In 1892 he had married a relative and—after the death of his father—Captain Mildmay (as he was known) followed the life of a country landowner, becoming a Justice of the Peace and member of the recently-formed Somerset County Council. He had a variety of interests, ranging from hunting and riding to drawing and painting. He also indulged a passion for planting flowering trees and shrubs, many of which in their maturity grace Hollam grounds today.

Captain Mildmay died in 1923, one year after the marriage of his second surviving daughter, Letitia (Letty), to Commander Denys Shoppee, R.N. Hollam House, as shown opposite, was rebuilt in Victorian times on the site of an older building, but after the second world war was partly pulled down and much altered in size and shape.

Locke—Wills—Clayton

In 1859 John Arthur Locke built Northmoor House for his bride, Adele Caroline Drewe, of Broadhembury, Devon. They had eight children and it was said that, every time a new baby was born, Mr. Locke added a new room to his large rambling residence which lies NW of Dulverton, off the road leading up to Five Crossways and Anstey Common. When the family was growing up, Mr. Locke

Hollam House.

employed the Rev. George Streynsham Jellicoe, M.A., of All Souls College, Oxford, to tutor his boys and act as chaplain to the new chapel-of-ease that he built at Marsh Bridge, and described as a 'plain building consisting of chancel, nave and turret with one bell, and four stained glass windows'. Jellicoe was an athletic chap, a relative of the Admiral, who built a 'clammer' or plank bridge across the river at Hinam, and afterwards called 'Jellicoe's Clammer'. Mr. Locke was a keen fisherman and hunting man himself, and kept a pack of harriers at Northmoor, providing his children with all the pleasures of country life. His son, Alec, became a parson, first working in London, and then held the living at Carhampton-cum-Rodhuish, where life in a country parish some seventy years ago was vividly described by his daughter, Anne, in the *Exmoor Review 1981*.

Mr. Locke died in 1888, but the chapel remained until about the year 1900, when it was mysteriously destroyed by fire. According to the *Free Press,* a Dulverton man happened to be passing and saw smoke coming out of the chapel. The alarm was raised, but the fire engine took so long to arrive and, 'being Saturday night', no one, was able to direct the hose with precision—some said it was never connected up! All that was left in the end was a few foundations, soon hidden by grass. But the fire was providential in that the Vicar of Dulverton regarded the chapel as an illegal intrusion, which detracted from his living. Certainly, so far out of town, it would have been difficult to maintain.

The next owner of Northmoor was the tobacco magnate, Sir Frederick Wills, whose son, Gilbert, built the Parish Rooms in Dulverton. Although the latter's wife thought that Dulverton was not 'good enough', her husband took the title when elevated to the peerage; and the present Lord Dulverton retains his interest in the locality.

In 1926 Northmoor came into the possession of Colonel Edward and Mrs. Clayton. Col. Clayton served as chairman of Somerset County Council after the war; and his son, David, has played a prominent part in local affairs as a business man, churchwarden, and district councillor.

View of Northmoor House (top left), woods, and chapel-of-ease at Marsh Bridge by the River Barle.

German

Building and estate workers at Northmoor House.

Marsh Bridge and Chapel.

Mardon—Green

Ashwick was one of several houses built in or near Dulverton, 80-100 years ago, by families who had made money—not in farming or landowning but in industry—and who, thanks to rapid transport by rail (and later by car), were able to build 'second' or retirement homes far from the towns where they normally lived and worked. Ashwick, about five miles NW of Dulverton Station, was one such example.

The house was built about the turn of the century by Heber Mardon, whose family had originated in Devon. In 1845, however, Heber's father had taken over a Bristol printer in settlement of a debt and turned it into a prosperous business—Mardon, Son & Hall—which eventually became the printing component of the Imperial Tobacco Company. Of brick and tile, the house was substantial rather than beautiful: with 8 'best' bedrooms, 5 servants' bedrooms, hall, 3 reception and one billiard room, all domestic offices, up-to-date lighting, heating and sanitary fittings, a water supply, and 'speaking tubes'. Attached were stabling, cottages and gardens, all contained within 44 acres of grounds. Then or later were acquired three farms (Mounsey, Ashwick and Slade), fishing on 1¾ miles of the river Barle, and shooting rights rented over 1400 acres of surrounding land. Hunting, too, was available with the Devon and Somerset Staghounds and other packs. In 1921 the Ashwick estate of 774 acres came on to the market and was offered as a whole for £18,000. In fact, it was sold off in lots, and that was how, a few years later, it came into the hands of an extraordinary character, Frank Green.

The Greens resembled the Mardons in that they too had made their money in industry, in their case at Wakefield in Yorkshire. In 1845 Frank's grandfather, Edward, had patented a Fuel Economiser which, in the century that followed, was sold all over the world for use in ships, power stations, and other industrial plants. Edward's son (another Edward) and grandson, Frank, played their part in the business, the latter acting as chairman of the company 1923-47, when his great-nephew, Colonel Simon Green, took over after war service in the Middle East.

The Ashwick connection came about in this manner. In 1924 Frank set off with a fleet of motorised caravans to tour Europe, but was unable to find a ship large enough to take them across the Channel. Looking around for somewhere to store them, he bought a 40-acre field on Mounsey Hill, near Ashwick, still known today as the 'Cara Field', where he put them in a shed. Three years later he fell seriously ill and was advised to live further south than Yorkshire, which led his

Ashwick House in 1984.

Ashwick Theatre or Music Room in 1984.

V.B-C.

V.B-C.

thoughts back to the caravans, at which time also Ashwick House happened again to be on the market. He promptly bought it, also Ashway Side, Ashway Farm, and various intervening lands; and in due course most of the properties that had constituted the original estate.

Frank was a man of eccentric habits and generous impulses. He had a passion for hunting, installed gates wherever helpful to the Hunt (irrespective of who owned the land), and likewise removed wire fences at will. He built stables at strategic spots, e.g. at Chibbet Post and Sandyway, and employed a gang of workmen to do a variety of jobs—from pulling ragwort and digging up docks, to peeling tarmac off a favourite cobbled road. With three Rolls Royces and a string of grooms on horses out hunting, he behaved like some latter-day pasha. During the war he refused to comply with an order to plough some land at Room Hill; whereupon the 'War Ag' ploughed it themselves but failed to put in a crop. On the other hand Frank was generous to friends, and built a small theatre or music room in a field near the house for the benefit of young relatives and staff, and allowed them to have parties there.

He did good service for the protection of Exmoor ponies. When he bought Ashwick, the Acland Herd had the right of 'free warren'. i.e. they ran wild over his land and the adjacent moorland on Winsford Hill. Frank arranged with the Acland Estate to act as the ponies' custodian and saw to it, for example, that they had hay in bad weather. During the war he did what he could to stop thieves coming down from the Midlands to round up the animals and butcher them for meat. After the war he made over part of his Ashwick property to his great-great-niece, Rose (now Mrs. Wallace). As she was still a girl, her father, Colonel Green, assisted in sorting out the best of the pure-bred mares (about a dozen), in which task he was given good help by the Westcott family of Draydon Farm. This was the foundation of the recovery of the Herd, and which—thanks to this action and careful culling and control—has now regained its place and reputation in the Herd Book. Frank finally retired to live at The Green in Dulverton, where he died in 1954 at the age of 93.

3 Victorian and Edwardian Dulverton

Between the 1850s and the 1880s the prosperity of Dulverton and neighbourhood depended, as it always had, on the state of farming and landowning. On the land generally this was the period of 'high farming'. Profits were ploughed into buildings, machinery, improved strains of cattle (notably the Red Devons pioneered by the Quartly family of Molland), and of sheep (e.g. the Bampton Notts or Devon Closewools and Exmoor Horns). But there was one important qualification. Whereas the owner and occupier did pretty well, the labourer was less fortunate. In 1860 the average weekly wage was 11s. 6d., in 1870 12s 2d. In winter and at other slack times, earnings were less. And whereas skilled men, such as carters, shepherds and gamekeepers were paid a few shillings extra, most labourers had to rely on their wives going out to work, and even on their children, in or out of school, to do the same. That, of course, was one of the main motives for poaching, and there were plenty of poachers round Dulverton, of whom 'Lordy Holcombe' was perhaps the best known.

On the other hand most small businesses and self-employed craftsmen made a reasonable living; and they played an important part in village life. A fair idea of Dulverton and around can be gleaned from the entries in *Kelly's Directory* of 1861. The immediate impression is that, with a population of 1,552 and a variety of jobs and trades, Dulverton was commercially prosperous and socially stable. The rural hierarchy was well entrenched. At the head of the list we find the names of six landowners, closely followed by those of about a dozen gentry and professional men. Among the latter was the Vicar, the Rev. Nathaniel Wodehouse, and his curate, the Rev. Henry John Taylor. The living was worth £330 p.a., with a vicarage and about 40 acres of glebe. Also three surgeons, as they were called, notably Dr. Charles Palk Collyns, who lived at Bilboa in the High Street (where the surgery still is), who acted as registrar for births and deaths, and whose classic work on the wild red deer was due to be published in the following year. Lastly we find the names of two solicitors, one of whom, Samuel Henry Warren, acted as clerk both to the Board of Guardians (responsible for the workhouse) and to the magistrates.

The main list, entitled 'Commercial' and arranged in alphabetical order, contained the names of 22 farmers and one 'cowkeeper', 9 innkeepers, 2 vets, 2 butchers, 2 saddlers and harness-makers, one blacksmith, one plumber, one wheelwright, one carpenter, one auctioneer and appraiser (valuer), 2 bakers, and 2 carriers. There were some interesting combinations. James Pearse was a saddler/harness maker, ironmonger and stationer. He was also agent for three insurance companies and kept the Post Office (letters arrived from Tiverton at 7.50 a.m. and were dispatched at 6.15 p.m.). At the (Red) Lion, Robert Slade kept an inn and posting house. Edwin Catford was a tailor and hatter. John Bradley, one of the vets, was relieving officer for the poor. The Clarke brothers were drapers and grocers. Charles Follett was a saddler and ironmonger. Edward Heath was a marine store dealer— euphemism for fishing tackle? John Ocock was a grocer and druggist. George Prideaux, plumber, was the parish clerk. Robert Warren was the miller at the Town Mills, who also baked bread. Henry German operated as a carrier, three days a week, from his house to Tiverton and back.

The largest business in the town was Warden & Co's 'Crape' Mill, powered by a waterwheel on the leat that left the river Barle in Lady Street and drove Robert Warren's twin breast wheels at the Town Mills on the way. 'Crape' or crepe making gave work to as many as 70 people at times. There were two other mills. One called the Paper Mill, long disused, was in Lady Street. The other, the Lower Mill—near the point where the leat rejoined the river Barle—was a grist mill in the hands of Henry Scott. In addition to these businesses there was a police station 'under the superintendence of Mr. Giddy, of Wiveliscombe'; the 'union' workhouse beside the river Barle; and 'schools now building'. All Saints' Church had been re-built in 1855 at a cost of £3,200 and was capable of accommodating 750 persons; and there was also the Independent Chapel in Milhams Lane founded in 1831. Market day was on Saturday, 'but only for the sale of killed meat'; while the two fairs took place in July and November as in the past. Dr. Sydenham remembered the last fair ever held in Dulverton—in 1874, by which time Lord Carnarvon had built a toll-free market near his new hotel in Brushford.

In the late 1870s radical changes began to overtake farming. There was a series of bad harvests, but any rise in the price of grain was forestalled by a flood of cheap corn grown in the newly-broken prairies of North America, and so the bottom fell out of corn production. Livestock was barely affected at first; but by 1890 even that market was going downhill, thanks to the advent of refrigeration and imports of chilled meat from the Americas and Australasia. The effect on hill farming round Dulverton was to make it yet more difficult, especially for the small occupier, to make ends meet. Heavy rainfall, high winds, and poor peaty soil were natural hazards he had had always to contend

Early view of Carnarvon Arms Hotel and Dulverton Station.

German

with; but the collapse of prices endangered his very survival. That many farmers did survive was due either to remissions of rent, the growth of dairying, or the fact that most hill farms rearing beef and sheep were family concerns, employing a minimum of paid labour and practising a way of life that approached actual self-sufficiency. All this had a knock-on effect on village life.

It was not, however, all gloom since, towards the end of the century, other sources of income began to come along. Richer folk had long spent the sporting season, or part of it, staying at country houses or putting up at hotels such as the (Red) Lion and the Lamb in Dulverton; but, owing to indifferent roads and the lack of public transport, the 'field' was largely local. Hunting depended almost entirely on the efforts and resources of private individuals: for instance on Mordaunt Fenwick Bisset, who, after a long lean period, revived the Devon and Somerset Staghounds and built the kennels at Exford; on J. Froude Bellew, who kept the foxhounds at Rhyll; and on J. A. Locke, who ran

29

the harriers from Northmoor. Once, however, the Taunton–Barnstaple railway had been completed in November, 1873, and the Exe Valley line had reached Dulverton (at Brushford) in August, 1884, the influx of visitors grew apace, and made possible a brisk horse bus service between the station and the town.

It was to encourage this trade that the Carnarvon Arms Hotel was built at Brushford in 1873-4, offering 'hunters and horses' and 'five miles of fishing on the Barle and Exe'. Trout fishing attracted a regular clientele between March and September, the rivers being stocked by—among others—the Exe Valley Fisheries, which had been started by an enterprising farmer who dug out some ponds in his fields at Exebridge in the 1880s. The business was taken over in 1900 and prospered under T. F. Tracey, a skilled trout breeder, who had learned the art at an old-established trout farm at Braunton in North Devon.

Field sports therefore were an important part of the growing trade of tourism, and they helped sustain certain kinds of village business. The 1902 *Kelly's,* for instance, listed 7 boot and shoemakers, 4 tailors and dressmakers, 3 saddlers and harness-makers, and 2 or more blacksmiths. Orders were generally bespoke, and most workshops employed several hands. There were also a photographer, J. H. German, an umbrella repairer, and a branch of the National Provincial Bank. In 1914 *Kelly's* recorded some significant changes: among them, the Dulverton Electric Lighting Company and, at Brushford, the Carnarvon Arms Garage which was open 'day, night and on Sundays'; also a market garden and nursery, and Goodlands, coal and builders' merchants, who relied entirely on the railway for the reception of heavy items such as fuel, bricks, cement, etc.

As to public life, parish councils and the rural district council had replaced the vestry by the Local Government Act 1894. A Bible Christian (Methodist) Chapel had been added to the places of worship in 1902, also a Library and Reading Room, all in Lady Street. A detachment of Volunteers had been converted into Territorials. The Dulverton Friendly Society still flourished, but its purposes would gradually be replaced by welfare legislation introduced by the Liberal Government. There were plenty of clubs—for bicycling, golf, football, cricket, also a glee club and a band.

Before the first world war, Dulverton, Bury, Brushford and Exebridge displayed a remarkably vigorous and varied country life as it used to be. But 1914-18 was the rubicon. Between the wars the countryside underwent far-reaching changes—some good, some deplorable—but they cannot be described in detail here. That story is implicit in all the photographs and information contributed by the many people who have helped in the making of this book.

Carnarvon Arms Hotel outside staff, and station bus.

Carnarvon Arms Garage. First proprietors, the Spencer brothers.

Bodger

4 *Dulverton — street by street*

Collecting photographs of Old Dulverton proved difficult for one reason only; for, thanks to generous help from numerous friends, we collected *too many*. What follows therefore is a *selection*, not a comprehensive *collection*, presented street by street. See Map on the inside front cover.

Battleton — Barle Bridge — Bridge Street

As you approach Dulverton from Brushford, you come first to Battleton, which consists of a long string of houses on either side of the road. Further on, at the junction with the road coming down Andrew's Hill on the left, is an elegant white 18th century building, Battleton House, once the home of Dr. G. F. Sydenham (1861-1924), respected medical officer and member of one of the oldest families in the neighbourhood, see pages 11-13. Beyond this house on the right is the Recreation Ground with its shelter, once the cattle pound for stray animals. It was presented to the town in 1920 by Charles Hardcastle Abbot as a memorial to the dead of the first world war. Pound Walk, a path along the river, leads up to the five-arched Barle bridge, which is probably more than 200 years old, see the picture on the front cover. In the great flood of 1952, which destroyed much of Lynmouth on the north coast, a 15-foot wall of water rushed south towards Dulverton, swept away a cottage on the near side of the bridge, caused havoc to buildings on the town side, and surged up to the top of Bridge Street.

Over Barle Bridge, away to the left, is a long lawn, at the end of which stands Exmoor House, now the headquarters of the Exmoor National Park Authority, formerly Dulverton Workhouse, built in 1855. Close by are the new buildings associated with the police and the fire service, which stand on the site of the allotments of the former Dulverton Friendly Society, now disbanded, see page 78.

Bridge Street runs up from Barle bridge towards the centre of the town, as far as Chapel Street on the right and the approach to the Town Mills on the left. After that it becomes High Street.

Opposite: Battleton decorated for Queen Victoria's Golden Jubilee, 1887.

German

Dr. G. F. Sydenham.

German

34 Early view of Battleton.

Bedwell

Battleton House on left. Cottage on right has disappeared.

Steer

On left, Cattle Pound (now Recreation Ground) and Pound Walk alongside the River Barle. In foreground, part of Dr. Sydenham's garden. On right, outflow of leat behind low wall. Dulverton in background.

Puttock

Exmoor House in 1984. Built as a Workhouse in 1855.

V.B-C.

36   Bridge Street looking towards Barle Bridge. On left, cottage destroyed by fire in 1918 (see opposite). On right, Bridge Inn and (with creeper) Boot Inn. Behind them is an area called 'The Castle', once a row of ancient cottages, with a cobbled footway, stream, and courtyard: replaced by Council Houses in 1926.

German

The fire was started, it was said, by a lad throwing paraffin on the hearth. The conflagration destroyed the cottage and adjoining properties (see below), which included a carpenter's shop, dairy, and slaughterhouse. The hand-operated fire engine was of little avail.

German/Bodger

Town Mills — Chapel Street

Between Bridge Street and High Street, and approximately at right angles to them are two lanes: on the south side, Chapel Street, once known as Duck Paddle; on the north side, the approach to Town Mills alongside the leat that used to drive four mills in Dulverton. The first of these was the Paper Mill in Lady Street, see page 72. The second was the Town Mills (plural because of twin breast wheels), owned by the Warren family for at least a hundred years. Robert Warren was recorded as a miller and baker in *Kelly's* 1861, and his descendants continued as millers until the house and buildings were acquired by the Rural District Council in 1973. They are now in private hands again, but not in use as a mill for the waterwheel was sold to Bickleigh Craft Centre, near Tiverton.

Robert Warren's grandson, Jack, helped by his sisters, Minnie and Blanche, worked all his life at milling. The leat had always to be kept clear of obstructions, and the sluice gates tarred and greased once a year. Hard corn from Russia and Canada was forwarded from Avonmouth to Dulverton station, two miles away, and fetched by Jack with horse and cart (later by lorry), sometimes up to five loads a day. A horse could draw up to 1½ tons. The grain then had to be ground, bagged, weighed and delivered in 2 cwt. sacks to farmers, who mixed it for cattle feed. Few customers bought flour for making bread. Grindstones of granite (usually French) lasted a lifetime, but might cost £400-£500 a pair when new. A millwright came out at intervals from Barnstaple to dress all the stones in the neighbourhood. The gearing was made of apple or holly wood (oak would split), so Jack would cut odd lengths off fallen apple trees, to replace worn cogs, at farms he used to visit.

The third mill was in Chapel Street and is now the Dulverton Laundry. This imposing three-storey building, supported by six vertical blocks of masonry running from ground to roof, may be over 200 years old and is an interesting example of an early Industrial Revolution factory. Originally a woollen mill making cloth and blankets, by the 1830s it was manufacturing 'crape' and employing up to 70 hands. Later crepe gave way to lace, and when that ended the building was used as a joinery, turning out doors and window frames. In the later 1800s it came into the hands of the Puttock family, first Peter Puttock, then his son Arthur, who used the waterwheel to drive his planes and saws. By the early 1900s the western end of the building and an adjoining outhouse were in use as a laundry, of which Arthur's wife, Elizabeth, took charge. Big coppers were used for boiling, and

Broomfield's Bakery, now a private house.

V.B-C.

mangles wrung the water out of the clothes and sheets, which were then hand-ironed. In 1935 the business was sold to Rodney Peake and his sister, Maria, who installed modern machinery and added a dry cleaning department. The waterwheel was cut up and disposed of. Frank Adams, who drove one of the delivery vans after the war, remembers how the business steadily expanded, so that by the time he retired he was calling on customers all over Exmoor. Under the present owners, Mr. and Mrs. Underhill, the laundry remains the principal industrial employer in Dulverton.

The fourth mill on the leat was Lower Mill, now a private residence. It was operated for grist by the Scott family until the 1920s, and by William Gibbons in the 1930s. The latter also had Oakford Mill, near Tiverton, which remained in full use for several years after the war in the charge of William's son, Hugh.

The first house in Chapel Street, on the right, was Broomfield's bakery. George Bryant started work there as a boy in 1921 for a wage of 5s. a week. The day started at 6.0 a.m. with the lighting of the faggot to fire the oven. Two batches of white bread were baked every day, 2lb. and 4lb. loaves. Delivery was by a two-wheel trolley, which meant hard work pushing it up Vicarage Hill; or further afield on horseback with the bread basket strapped to the rider's back. On Sundays family dinners were baked between 11.0 a.m. and 1.0 p.m. for 2d. a time. Other bakeries, such as Darch's in Fore Street, did the same.

Chapel Street took its name from the Independent or Congregational Chapel at the far end of the street, at the junction with Milhams Lane. See page 43.

Town Mills. The leat runs beyond the wall on the left.

Hawtin

Great spur wheel, wallower (below), pit wheel behind.

Laundry building, formerly crepe mill.

Laundry staff before 1914. Mrs. Elizabeth Puttock seated on right.

V.B-C.

41

Chilcott

Lower Mill, the fourth mill driven by the Dulverton leat, now a private house.

V.B-C.

42   Riverside House, next to Lower Mill. A social scene of much interest. Note the fashions, especially the pudding mould cap of the maid. Individuals not identified.

German

The Congregational Chapel was built in 1831 at the instance of the pastor, the Rev. W. Standerwich. The manse was added in 1877, at a cost of £358 15s., prompted by George Williams, founder of the Y.M.C.A. He performed the opening ceremony for the newly-built school hall and classrooms.

Hammer

High Street — Church Lane — Rosemary Lane

For convenience High Street can be divided into three sections. The first section runs up to the Lamb Hotel and can be studied on pages 44-47. The second section bears right at The Lamb and runs up to the car park, see page 48. The third section runs from the car park up to Vicarage Hill, at the junction with Church Lane and Rosemary Lane, see page 49.

High Street — first section

At the bottom, beside the leat, a shop projects into the road and was formerly occupied by Moore & Stimson, the largest tailor in Dulverton (see top photo opposite), some of whose staff can be seen in the bottom photo. There was a separate dressmaking department at the back. Other tailoring establishments in the town included those of Arthur Chilcott, Harding Perry (in Fore Street, see page 58) and Tom Price. These and other smaller workshops and several self-employed tailors and dressmakers absorbed some 50 people, who depended largely on orders received *every year* for new outfits for grooms and hunt servants, and on work sent down from London's Saville Row. The trade declined sharply after the first world war, and was virtually extinguished by the advent of cheap ready-to-wear clothing.

An early view of the police station at the junction between Fore Street and High Street: subsequently Ellerton's Stores, then a cycle shop, bank, and now a chemist.

Bodger

44

Looking uphill. Moore & Stimson, tailors, on left. Ellerton's Stores, centre background. Coal cart at entrance to Chapel Street on right. Note rough road surface.

Puttock

Staff of Moore & Stimson in their best clothes. Mr. Moore lived at The Retreat, next to the present Roman Catholic Church.

German

Ellerton's Stores, now a chemist, in centre, Lamb Hotel on right. Below the hotel were some bushes where, as a small boy, Ivan Kemp used to hide in fear of Sir Gilbert Wills's black valet, who used to ride a fast motor-cycle into town.

Bodger

Goodlands coal cart.

Rendell

Looking downhill. Top left the Lamb Hotel, once called the Ram; then Thorne's, drapers, formerly the post office kept by Edwin Catford; then a house claimed as the original of The White Horse in *Lorna Doone,* occupied first by Chilcott, tailor, subsequently by Yerbury, bespoke shoemaker, who had started life as a Barnardo boy and was trained to make artificial limbs in the first world war. Top right can be seen the premises of W. & L. How, grocers; Ernest Kemp, dairy; Harry Tout, who sold fishing tackle, cycles and two-gallon cans of petrol (the first man in Dulverton to do so; his shop was taken over by Henry Mainerd, hairdresser); next door, a cafe kept by Miss Radley; then two businesses invisible in this picture—Frayne, a shoemaker, and a grocery which became Hammond's bakery. In the street outside the cafe once stood a standpipe for fresh water. In the centre, at the bottom (in Moore & Stimson's old premises) lived Arthur J. Court, a grocer who switched to antiques and auctioneering. His wife was a dressmaker and sold ladies' footwear. On the hill in the background is The Cottage, for many years the home of the Abbot family, renowned for its azaleas and rhododendrons that still make a brilliant splash of colour in the spring.

Somerset County Record Office

47

High Street — second section

Above the Lamb Hotel is an opening that gives access to Crispin's, once a group of old cottages and now converted into a restaurant. Next to it is a drive that leads to The Green (see below), latterly known as The Greenway, a period house that has served in the past as a parsonage, hotel, private house, and is now divided into flats. Further up the street, on the right, is an alleyway with the sinister name of Hangman's Alley, reason unknown. Opposite, on the left, are the backs of the buildings in Fore Street and the Town Hall.

The car park was occupied for many years by the Lion Hotel stables ('Lion Hunting Stables'), with a number of horseboxes in the charge of Bill Hancox, and in full use for hunting and hacking. Another Dulverton character, Charlie Hoskins, jobmaster, also kept a horse there. He drove one of the station buses (his rival, Danny Roberts, drove the other). Earlier still had been 'Larcombe's Van', driven by Tom Slape, who would carry anything from paraffin to bacon, and park his vehicle behind Darch's bakery in Fore Street. No traffic troubles then!

The Green, when used as an hotel.

Vowles

Sydenham Hall.

V.B-C.

High Street — third section

The right-hand side of this section, once called Back Street, has seen many changes: including a dairy (now Tout's accessories); a stationer-cum-chemist (now Kemp's Newsagency); the offices of the solicitors, Barrow & Chapman (now a picture shop); Bilboa house, unchanged as a doctor's residence with a modern surgery next door; the New Inn (now a private house); and at the corner of Rosemary Lane, Billy Arnold's sweet shop (long gone). On the left-hand side at the bottom were successively a butcher, Goodland (now an estate agent); a tailor, Tom Price (now a boutique); and further up the street Sydenham Hall, possibly the original manor house of the Sydenham family. It was once described as 'the old mansion that stood almost in the centre of the town and, with its grounds, covered a large part of the triangle interposed between High Street and Market (i.e. Bank) Square. Long and low, the front was for most purposes the back, the great entrance being on the garden side.' Inside the house was said to be a 'praying cupboard, complete with elbow rests and space for a crucifix'. At the top end of the street was Thorne's bakery and Eli Fisher, a provisions merchant.

Across the top of High Street are two narrow lanes. Church Lane (see right), partly cobbled, has several old cottages, one with a mason's sign over the door. Another—perhaps a pair—may have been the parish poorhouse. Wood's Cafe, now in Bank Square, started here as No. 1. The Hollam Brook has always run underneath the pathway. Owing to a long history of flooding, work began in 1985 to divert the flow into a piped channel. Below, Rosemary Lane runs beside the Vicarage wall as far as the Parish Rooms, built in 1912 by Sir Gilbert Wills, where the Exmoor Society has its office on the first floor. Budds House in the corner was once a farm.

50

V.B-C.

Looking up Vicarage Hill. In centre, the Rock Inn.

Persehouse

Vicarage Hill — Jury Road — Town Marsh

The photograph above is an early one, taken from the top of High Street, and shows the short stretch of steepish road known as Vicarage Hill, with Rock (House) inn in the background. On the left is the shop belonging to Eli Fisher, who sold provisions and boots and shoes, an odd combination, but there was a reason. Eli had been a postman: which meant that, like George Bickell, he would walk out with the morning mail to one or two outlying villages, and stay there until coming back with the evening dispatch. In the middle of the day, he would retire to a bothy and mend shoes, hence his interest in selling footwear. On the right is Billy Arnold's sweet shop (where you could buy 'ha'penny reds'), the turning into Rosemary Lane, and the Vicarage wall. No pavement runs beside the wall as now, but note the standpipe and lamp standard. The lamp was lit by oil housed in a metal well with a globe encasing the wick. As it grew dark, Charles Wensley and George Puttock used to go round the town with ladders and light up all the lamps. At 10.0 p.m. they doused them all with 'a long curved tube, the end of which curled down into the globe or bowl'.

At the far end of the wall, Turnpike Cottage can just be seen. A turnpike stood there in 1820 and probably later, but the cottage was pulled down in the 1920s. The site now forms part of the wall round Woodcote, a house built in the early 1920s by Gerard Luard, a London solicitor. Round the corner in Jury Road are two very old colour-washed cottages, Woodliving and Woodside, with tall exterior chimneys abutting the road, and thought to date from the late 16th/early 17th centuries. One of them contains plaster panels, highly painted with multi-coloured geometrical patterns. These two dwellings probably marked the limits of Old Dulverton on the road to Minehead, with the tanyard beyond. To the left of the Rock Inn are two lanes—one running up to Hollam, the other to Town Marsh, see pages 54-57.

This photograph shows Hollam Cottage with annexe (a separate dwelling, now gone). In centre is Hollam Lane, where stand a butcher's or baker's roundsman and, behind him, Jimmy Saunders (in apron), a saddler with premises in the corner of the Rock Inn on right. The opening to the left of Hollam Cottage leads to the Town Marsh.

Chilcott

52

Woodleigh, Dulverton.

Jury Road starts at the Rock Inn and leads uphill past Woodcote to two historic old thatched cottages, Woodliving and Woodside, sometimes called Woodleigh.

Hole

Looking back towards Vicarage Hill. On left is Woodcote. On right, Turnpike Cottage which used to stand on the corner below Woodcote.

V.B-C./Bodger

Looking down Vicarage Hill. On right, Wreneaton House (with gables) and garden wall, now a garage area. Behind it a broad strip of land, known as Vicarage Orchard, ran from Church Lane (to right of dark figure) up to Town Marsh, so-called because of the periodical flooding by the Hollam Brook which flowed through it. When the water rose too high, Mr. Hobbs, the Council foreman, would insert a fender and divert the flood water over Vicarage Hill. The Brook, however, served several useful purposes. It probably flushed the lavatories in the town and, ponded upstream, drove the water wheel attached to the Town Smithy, see p. 56. This was worked for many years by the Govier family, who specialised in sharpening and making edge tools, such as sickles and scythes.

Puttock

Opposite is a view towards Town Marsh cottages from the Hollam Lane area, parish church in background, Marsh Hall in foreground behind the trees.

Puttock

Town Marsh cottages with Reg Pike, groom at Pixton, on horse, and Fred Govier, blacksmith.

Hodge

Town Marsh Smithy.

Warren

Marsh Hall, built in 1884 as the Gospel Hall by the Mildmay family for evangelical worship, principally by the Plymouth Brethren. It is now the property of the Dulverton Seniors' Club.

V.B-C.

Thatcher at work, Town Marsh.

Hodge

Looking up Fore Street, c. 1900. On left, Summers, butcher; Bayley, grocer and draper; Follett, saddler (in present post office building). On right Market House (later the Town Hall); and, just visible, the station bus.

Somerset County Record Office

Fore Street — Bank Square — All Saints' Church

Today Fore Street is a pleasant wide street, but it must have looked very empty in the past—as in the above photograph from the Somerset County Records Office—except on market day, or on the two annual fairs in July and November, or whenever the staghounds met in the town, or on festive occasions such as Queen Victoria's Jubilees in 1887 and 1897 (see opposite). Originally there were no shops at the bottom of the street. On the left were an ironmonger/plumber (W. & L. German, a family business founded in 1847, still there today); a butcher (Uppington); a general stores (Benjamin Bayley) succeeded by Ellerton's, whose premises were burnt out on August Bank Holiday 1922 when the Exeter fire engine had to be summoned, see page 61. Further up, at the corner of Lady Street, were premises occupied by Charles Follett, saddler, now the post office. On the right, at the bottom, were a bakery (Darch), once an inn; a cycle and fishing tackle shop (Tout); the Market House, an 18th century building converted into the Town Hall and furnished in 1927 with exterior steps to the design of Professor Albert Richardson; a tailor, Harding Perry, nicknamed 'a quarter to three' by the way he walked with feet at 90 degrees; a jeweller (Venn); and finally the Lion Hotel Garage (Captain Popkiss), removed after the last war for street widening.

58

Bank Square closed the view across the top of Fore Street. As noted, the main entrance to Sydenham Hall in High Street used to go through from this side, before the bank was built. Looking downhill, on the left were Wood's cafe and bakery (still there but formerly in Church Lane or Street), and the Lion Hotel (once the Red Lion), whose proprietor in the 1870s-1880s was William King. At the sale in 1888 the property was described as having '16 bedrooms, coach houses, lofts, granary, stabling for 35 horses, and a walled garden fully stocked with fruit trees'. The bar today displays some interesting old photos and receipted bills. Many publicans used to do their own brewing, as did other people. The beer was taken round the houses in 4½-gallon firkins, and sold at 2d.–4d. a pint, according to quality. In the 1880s Dulverton had more than a dozen inns. On the opposite side of the Square stood private houses as now; and in the passageway below the churchyard the weaver's studio was originally built (with a fine north light) for John H. German, the Dulverton-born photographer, many of whose pictures illustrate this book.

Feast in honour of Queen Victoria's Diamond Jubilee, 1887, in Bank Square at top of Fore Street.

German 59

German Brothers, ironmoners, old-established family business. Note the display of oil lamps. Pre-1914.

Puttock

60

Ellerton's Stores, formerly in High Street, successors to Bayley's. The house is claimed as that of Reuben Huckaback in Blackmore's *Lorna Doone*. See opposite.

Hole

Exeter fire engine was summoned, among others, to help put out the fire at Ellerton's
Stores, on August Bank Holiday 1922. Note the studded wheels.

Bodger/Steer

Looking down Fore Street from Bank Square. On left, the Lion Hotel before addition of front gable and portico. Station bus under hotel sign. Follett, saddler, on right.

German

62

Artillery unit in Bank Square, before 1914. Wood's Cafe on left. Lion Hotel now has its front gable, portico, and lamp.

German

F. WOOD,

Baker and Confectioner.

1, **CHURCH STREET,**

DULVERTON.

From Rintouls, Brewer St., London, Gold & Silver Medallist Cookery & Food Exhibition, 1893.

Luncheon, Tea, Pound, Genoa, Seed, Madeira,
Birthday, Wedding, and other Cakes to order.

WHOLE MEAL BREAD, same as supplied to Royalty.

Fred Wood came from London about the turn of the century and started a bakery in Church Lane or Street. Later he moved to the present premises, known as Wood's Cafe and Balsom's Bakery. The building was originally used as a Dame School, attended as a child by George Williams, of Ashway Farm, founder of the Y.M.C.A.

Balsom

Weavers Studio in the passageway below the churchyard. It was built in the 1890s, with a fine north light, for the photographer, John H. German.

The parish church of All Saints, Dulverton, stands on the mound above Bank Square, a handsome building in mellow stone. The old church was virtually destroyed when the Victorians conducted a ruthless 'restoration' in 1853-55, but rebuilt on much the same plan as before, though wider and re-using the ancient columns. However, the losses included an ancient rood screen, tympanum, and galleries; only the west tower remained intact. In the last 100 years the interior has been re-furnished and re-decorated, with pulpit, font, much stained glass, and memorials to local families. The churchyard was fenced in 1856, and subsequently terraced and planted with bulbs that make a fine show in the spring. The old Belfry Tree, a sycamore, is now a stump, but a line of sturdy yews enhances the site and setting. In the vestry is the parish copy of the 1841 Tithe Map, which pulls down like a roller blind.

Vowles

Interior of All Saints after restoration, but before addition of new screen in early 1900s.

65

Church choir. Dr. Sydenham stands on left, George Bowbeer Fisher on right. Sitting in centre, the Rev. H. J. Green. c. 1916.

German

Lady Street — Northmoor Road

'Lady' is thought to have derived from a pre-Reformation statue of the Blessed Virgin Mary, that was placed either on an arch over the street or in a niche to one side. In the 1820 map it is called Lady's Street. Always narrow, it was once so closed-in that 'two putt carts could not pass'; and it still causes traffic problems.

On the west or lower side of the street were two important local enterprises, active for many years. One belonged to Robert Page, described in the advertisement below as a 'mechanical engineer', who made waterwheels and in-barn threshers, sawbenches and reed-makers, and later turned to building carriages and pony traps. After some 40 years, the business ceased trading in the 1920s. One of Mr. Page's descendants, Herbert, became chief clerk to the solicitors, Barrow & Chapman, and distinguished himself as a billiard player, winning the British Legion championship six times.

Behind Page's premises was the other enterprise—that of G. B. Fisher & Son, principal builders in the town. George Bowbeer Fisher was born in Dulverton in 1844. As a young man he went over to the USA, where he worked as a carpenter on the railroad then being built between Chicago and Kansas City. He returned to Dulverton in 1876

ROBERT PAGE,

Agricultural Implement Manufacturer,

MECHANICAL ENGINEER,

WHEELWRIGHT & BLACKSMITH,

Having purchased the old established Business of Mr. Quick, hopes, by strict personal attention, with the practical knowledge of the different branches, to secure a large share of support.

DULVERTON.

Notice in local newspaper of 1883.

Assembly loft and carpenter's shop.

Warren 67

Paint shop, later fire station.

PAGE'S PREMISES

Cast iron nameplate.

Smithy and forge.

George Bowbeer Fisher in his pony trap in Battleton.

Puttock

and, with the money he had made, started his own building business at a time when there were plenty of openings. He was concerned, for example, with the building of Northmoor Farm, Warmore House, Wreneaton, and additions to the Carnarvon Arms Hotel. He assembled a staff of 20-30, including eight carpenters making coffins, doors, and house fittings of every description. He was also one of the first to use electricity. His first generator may have been a Compton (75 volts 30 amps), driven by a steam engine, later replaced by an oil engine built by W. H. Pool & Sons, of Chipstable, that gave way in turn to a much larger plant installed in a shed now used for making kitchen units. Fisher was soon selling surplus current to private houses, the post office, Lion Hotel, etc., the charge being about one shilling a week for a maximum of three lights per house. He helped form the Dulverton Electric Light Company and instal a small hydro-electric plant on the river Barle, additional to the plant at his works. The two were maintained by Jack Davis, assisted by Guy Rendell, who together did all the repairs and line work, and dashed between the two units on bicycles. G. B. Fisher died in 1917 and was succeeded by his son, George Henry. After the latter's death in 1946, the business was sustained by a group of employees led by David Bodger, formerly a carpenter working with Robert Page.

George Henry's brother-in-law was George Arnold, who combined market gardening with milking cows in a dairy in Lady Street, which had been started by Fisher's during the first world war, and kept going by George's children, Jack and Joan Arnold, until 1976. The cows grazed the fields round the town, and were driven through Fore Street and other thoroughfares before and after milking—a familiar sight in Dulverton for many years.

Other features along Lady Street and its continuation as Northmoor Road are illustrated in the photographs that follow.

Railroad car (Chicago, Quincy, Kansas City) on which G. B. Fisher worked as a carpenter.

Arnold   69

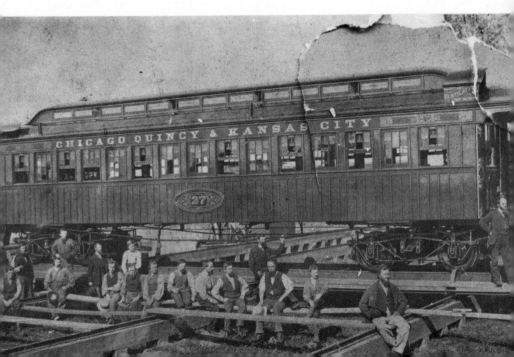

Further along Lady Street are the British Legion house; the police station and house built in 1903-4, now in private use; the Bible Christian (Methodist) Chapel built in 1902; and Paper Mill house incorporating a cottage known as The Birdcage, where Lady Street joins Northmoor Road. It seems that the Paper Mill itself was a separate building sited upstream, see p.72, while the present house may have once served as a grist mill. The picture above, taken in Northmoor Road, shows one of several bridges over the leat and looks back towards Paper Mill house, where it is linked by another bridge to an area of cottages and gardens. Here were Dart's Stables, see picture opposite, which supplied horses for the yeomanry as well as 'Good Hunters for Sale and Hire', notably to followers of the Devon and Somerset Staghounds, whose Boxing Day meet in Fore Street can be seen below.

Puttock/German   71

In centre, old Paper Mill building, now demolished. Strawberry
beds on hill on right.

German

Paper   Mill   house   (The
Birdcage).

V.B-C.

72

'The Vineyard' was the name given to part of the steep ground above Lady Street/ Northmoor Road, devoted to strawberry beds and a market garden, worked by Henry German, who also plied as a carrier between Dulverton and Tiverton, until the Exe Valley Railway 'rendered conveyance of passengers and goods more comfortable and expeditious'. Cultivation must have been arduous but carting manure up to the beds and removing the produce were facilitated by the use of a truck on rails, hauled up and down the steep slope by a winch operated by two men.

German

73

5 Some People and Events

Off to pick 'urts, c. 1916.

German

Dulverton fire engine, c. 1920s.

Seniors Club

Dulverton football team, 1906.

Dulverton Carnival, before 1914.

Postman John Bickell brought the letters from Dulverton to Winsford every day for forty years. Starting at 6.0 a.m. he walked over the hill to Chilly Bridge, along the Exe Valley road, and cut off another corner at Coupleham. During the day he worked at Mr. Dadds' boot repairing shop (now the Post Office) and walked back to Dulverton in the evening, carrying the Winsford mail. A purse of sovereigns was presented to him on his retirement on 22 October 1898. He died at Dulverton aged 84.

Town Hall, rebuilt with exterior steps, declared open, August 1927.

Sir John Hope Simpson, M.P., Liberal M.P. for Taunton, 1922-24.

Arnold

Puttock

Dulverton Friendly Society was founded in 1816 to provide sickness benefit for its members, who totalled 300 by 1897. Members paid one shilling monthly, and this income was augmented by a series of fines imposed for a wide variety of misdemeanours, e.g. arrears in subscriptions; stewards not visiting the sick or paying out their benefit; fighting and quarrelling at meetings; blaspheming or degrading the established religion or government; and working, hunting or fishing when supposed to be sick. Rents for gardens acquired in 1856 were also received. Out of these funds any member who fell sick was paid a generous 10 shillings 'bed' pay weekly, while the 'walking sick' received 5 shillings. Some payments were made to the 'aged', and a handsome contribution to funeral expenses of members and their wives, although the rules stated clearly that 'no man bury more than one wife at the expense of the Society'. An annual club walk was held on Whit-Monday when the Society banner was carried proudly at the head of the march—it had to be waved back and forth so that both sides of it might be seen clearly. A church service preceded a feast held usually at the (Red) Lion. The Society provided essential help during hard times; and only with the advent of the welfare state did it outlive its usefulness. It was disbanded in 1968, and the banner presented to the County Museum in Taunton, see above.

Western Morning News

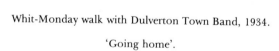

Whit-Monday walk with Dulverton Town Band, 1934.

'Going home'.

6 *Bury*

The name of this tiny hamlet of brown and white houses means 'fortified place'; and the outlines of a 'castle' can still be traced above the confluence of the Exe and Haddeo rivers. A bridleway runs alongside the Haddeo all the way up to Wimbleball Lake.

River Haddeo and Packhorse Bridge in 1985.

V.B-C.

School, then Anglican chapel, now a private house.

OLD BUILDINGS IN BURY

7 *Brushford*

Brushford has a distinct identity with a fine mediaeval church, old rectory, and cottages close by. Combe, seat of the Sydenhams, is also in the parish. Dulverton was the railway station here, on the Taunton-Barnstaple line, before Beeching closed it; but the Carnarvon Arms Hotel, built about the same time (1873), still flourishes.

Rectory behind the parish church of S. Nicholas, and old cottages in foreground.
Catford

Charles Chilcott and son, Arthur, with their milk float. The field behind is now the site of Council houses.
Chilcott

Carnarvon Arms Hotel, as originally built in 1873.

The hotel, after extension by the Pixton Estate.

Nelder/Jones

Carnarvon Arms Hotel, Dulverton, Exmoor.

Somerset County Show held at Newbridge c. 1905, and sponsored by Charles Nelder,
tenant of the Carnarvon Arms Hotel.

Dulverton–Lynmouth coach, outside the hotel.

Chilcott

German

Farmer Richard Hodge and his sister driving into Langaller Farm, c. 1926. Taunton-Barnstaple line in background.
Palmer

Dulverton railway station (at Brushford) in full use in 1963. Down train to Barnstaple in centre. Exe Valley branch on right.
Fox

8 *Exebridge*

Exebridge lies on both sides of the bridge that marks the boundary between Devon and Somerset. The hamlet is notable for Exe Valley Fisheries, Anchor Inn, a nursery, and sawmills.

Exebridge before 1914. Anchor Inn, centre right.

Bedwell

The former Toll House in 1985.

V.B-C.

Fry and yearling ponds at Exe Valley Fisheries in the 1930s.

Topical Press

Staff of Exebridge Sawmills (Messrs. Bartlett & Bayliss), before 1914.

Puttock

9 Memories and Acknowledgments

Facts can be looked up in books and documents, but the memories of living people must be searched before they forget what life was like in the past; indeed before death extinguishes those memories for ever. In our search we have relied in the main on assistance from men and women over the age of 60—some now, alas, no longer alive—with whom we have chatted and reminisced. The results were so bountiful that it became impossible to use more than a tenth of all the information and photographs we received. Nonetheless we would like to pay tribute to the following, listed alphabetically, while asking forgiveness from any whose names may inadvertently have been omitted.

Frank and Phyllis Adams, Joan Astell, Jack Arnold, Bernard Balsom, Jim Bodger, David Bromwich, Rev. Richard Brown, George Bryant, 'Nip' Chanter, Arthur Chilcott, Barbara Christopher, Elsie Clayton, George Coates, Mary Cross, Edgar German, Ron German, Maurice Gibson, Frank Hawtin, Alan Hearth, David and Jane Hill, Fred Hodge, Len How, Shirley Howard, David Hunt, Francois and Toni Jones (and other organisers of the Brushford Exhibition 1984), Isabelle Jones, Philip Jones, Ivan Kemp, Betty Mardon, Lt.-Col. J. K. La Touche Mardon, C. G. May, Roger Miles, Kathleen Nelder, Peggy Palmer, Mrs. Pershouse, Reg Puttock, Jimmy Quick, Bill Rendell, Elizabeth Robinson, Cecil Scoins, Winifred Smallridge, Charles, Florence and Alan Steer, Tom Stoneham, Marjorie Trelford, Derrick Warren, Jack and Minnie Warren, Rose Wallace and her father, Col. Simon Green, David Webb, Lil Webber, Clery Welch.

The Authors

Hilary Binding teaches at Minehead Middle School. With Douglas Stevens she wrote *A New History of Minehead* (1977), and is the author of the Microstudy, *Old Minehead and around* (1983). She and Victor Bonham-Carter have been joint editors of *The Exmoor Review* since 1981.

Victor Bonham-Carter is a professional author. In addition to journalism and broadcasting, he has written nine full-length books on rural, military and social subjects: the most recent being *Authors by Profession,* a two-volume history of the business of authorship since the introduction of printing. He is the President of the Exmoor Society.